W9-CGN-385

WALKING WITH GOD

QUOTATIONS FROM THE SERMONS OF
DR. CHARLES F. STANLEY

P.O. Box 7900, Atlanta, GA 30357
(800) 789-1473
intouch.org

Walking with God

Published in Nashville, Tennessee, by Thomas Nelson. Thomas Nelson is a registered trademark of HarperCollins Christian Publishing, Inc.

Note: The following quotations have been taken from the sermons of Dr. Charles F. Stanley as they were preached at the First Baptist Church in Atlanta, Georgia, and may contain slight differences from the published *Life Principles to Live By* audio and video series.

Thomas Nelson, Inc., titles may be purchased in bulk for educational, business, fund-raising, or sales promotional use. For information, please e-mail SpecialMarkets@ThomasNelson.com.

Scripture quotations are taken from the NEW AMERICAN STANDARD BIBLE®, © The Lockman Foundation 1960, 1962, 1963, 1968, 1971, 1972, 1973, 1975, 1977, 1995. Used by permission. www.Lockman.org

ISBN 978-0-529-11215-6

Printed in China

15 16 17 18 DSC 7 6 5 4

TABLE OF CONTENTS

Thank you for your faithful partnership in proclaiming the life-changing truth of the gospel to people around the world. Through God's grace, power, and provision, In Touch Ministries has been leading people into growing relationships with Jesus Christ for the last 35 years—and I believe the best is yet to come. I look forward to all He will do through our partnership in the years ahead.

I pray God will keep you safe, healthy, and in the center of His will. I also hope this book of quotations will encourage you as you walk with Him daily. May He richly bless you as you follow Him in obedience.

—Dr. Charles F. Stanley

Our intimacy with God—His highest priority for our lives—determines the impact of our lives.

O GOD, You are my God; I shall seek You earnestly;
My soul thirsts for You . . .
For You have been my help,
and in the shadow of Your wings I sing for joy.
My soul clings to You;
Your right hand upholds me.

—PSALM 63:1, 7-8

God has purposed to reproduce
His life in and through your life.
In order for that to happen,
He must reveal Himself to you
and bring you into an intimate
relationship with Himself.

DR. CHARLES F. STANLEY

God, who said, "Light shall shine out of darkness," is the One
who has shone in our hearts to give the Light of the knowledge of
the glory of God in the face of Christ. But we have this treasure
in earthen vessels, so that the surpassing greatness of the power
will be of God and not from ourselves.

—2 CORINTHIANS 4:6-7

Everyone has a direct relationship to God because of who He is. He is the Creator of this world and all that is in it. He is the sovereign Ruler of this entire universe. He is the Sustainer of everything, Provider for every need, and He is the Judge of all mankind.

DR. CHARLES F. STANLEY

 Since the creation of the world His invisible attributes, His eternal power and divine nature, have been clearly seen, being understood through what has been made, so that they are without excuse.

—ROMANS 1:20

On the basis of Christ's death,
you have been declared not
guilty. You have agreed that He
will pay your sin debt in full.
You have been reconciled—
no matter how sinful you've been.
He has brought you back into
relationship with Himself, and
the moment you trust Him as
your Savior, He sets you apart for
His purposes in life.

DR. CHARLES F. STANLEY

When you were dead in your transgressions and the uncircumcision
of your flesh, He made you alive together with Him, having forgiven us all
our transgressions, having canceled out the certificate of debt consisting
of decrees against us, which was hostile to us; and He has taken it out
of the way, having nailed it to the cross.

—COLOSSIANS 2:13-14

In the beginning God said, "Let Us make man in Our image." Why? So we can know Him, love Him, and receive His goodness and kindness. That is God's purpose.

DR. CHARLES F. STANLEY

God said, "Let Us make man in Our image,
according to Our likeness. . . ." God created man
in His own image, in the image of God He created
him; male and female He created them.

—GENESIS 1:26-27

Intimacy says, "God, here is my heart. I am willing to unwrap myself before You—my soul, my spirit, and everything I am. I want You to know there is nothing I am holding back." This is a personal relationship. This is true intimacy.

DR. CHARLES F. STANLEY

 Search me, O God, and know my heart;
try me and know my anxious thoughts;
and see if there be any hurtful way in me,
and lead me in the everlasting way.

—PSALM 139:23-24

God wants you to know Him fully.
He created you so that He could
reveal Himself to you and express
His love through you.

DR. CHARLES F. STANLEY

 "Know therefore that the LORD your God, He is God,
the faithful God, who keeps His covenant and His
lovingkindness to a thousandth generation with those
who love Him and keep His commandments."

—DEUTERONOMY 7:9

Obey God and leave all the consequences to Him.

Peter and the apostles answered, "We must obey God rather than men. The God of our fathers raised up Jesus, whom you had put to death by hanging Him on a cross. He is the one whom God exalted to His right hand as a Prince and a Savior, to grant repentance to Israel, and forgiveness of sins. And we are witnesses of these things; and so is the Holy Spirit, whom God has given to those who obey Him."

—ACTS 5:29-32

Those of us who are followers
of Jesus Christ should be very
interested in the consequences of
our actions because they will have
impact either for good or evil.

DR. CHARLES F. STANLEY

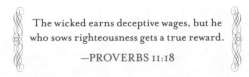

The wicked earns deceptive wages, but he
who sows righteousness gets a true reward.

—PROVERBS 11:18

Everyone makes decisions
that impact his or her life—
and the consequences of those
decisions spill over into the lives
of others. That is why you can't
say, "It's my own life, I will do
with it whatever I please."
You and I can't live that way
because we all have influence.

DR. CHARLES F. STANLEY

 All the paths of the LORD are lovingkindness and truth
to those who keep His covenant and His testimonies.

—PSALM 25:10

You will not make wise decisions
in life unless you wholeheartedly
believe this one basic, theological
fact—God is absolutely sovereign.

DR. CHARLES F. STANLEY

 The LORD has established His throne in the heavens,
and His sovereignty rules over all.

—PSALM 103:19

You and I may not know or understand all the reasons why God allows certain things to happen. He doesn't promise us that. What He guarantees us is that whatever we face in life, He is going to be with those of us who are His children.

DR. CHARLES F. STANLEY

"Be strong and courageous, do not be afraid or tremble at them, for the LORD your God is the one who goes with you. He will not fail you or forsake you."

—DEUTERONOMY 31:6

If I expect God to turn all the circumstances of my life into something good, then I must be willing to trust Him, love Him, and surrender all to Him.

DR. CHARLES F. STANLEY

"You whom I have taken from the ends of the earth, and called from its remotest parts and said to you, 'You are My servant, I have chosen you and not rejected you. Do not fear, for I am with you; do not anxiously look about you, for I am your God. I will strengthen you, surely I will help you, surely I will uphold you with My righteous right hand.'"

—ISAIAH 41:9-10

You can never go wrong obeying God. Why? Simply because you do not know what the consequences of your obedience will be, but He does— and they are always good.

DR. CHARLES F. STANLEY

"Obey My voice, and I will be your God, and you will be My people; and you will walk in all the way which I command you, that it may be well with you."

—JEREMIAH 7:23

God's Word is an immovable anchor in times of storm.

This hope we have as an anchor of the soul, a hope both sure and steadfast and one which enters within the veil, where Jesus has entered as a forerunner for us, having become a high priest forever.

—HEBREWS 6:19-20

If God ignites a storm in your life,
He has a definite purpose in mind
for it. Even if the difficulties you
face don't come from Him, He
takes advantage of them and makes
them profitable for you.

DR. CHARLES F. STANLEY

 Whatever was written in earlier times was written for
our instruction, so that through perseverance and the
encouragement of the Scriptures we might have hope.

—ROMANS 15:4

A storm can either destroy you
or develop you. If you are truly
submitted to God, He will use
the storms you encounter in life
to build your strength, wisdom,
knowledge, understanding,
commitment, devotion, faith,
serenity, peace, and joy.

DR. CHARLES F. STANLEY

 It is good for me that I was afflicted, that I may learn
Your statutes. The law of Your mouth is better to me
than thousands of gold and silver pieces.

—PSALM 119:71-72

The Word of God is our anchor.
Storms in life are inevitable, but
our anchor is immovable and
unchanging. It holds us solidly to
the rock of Christ.

DR. CHARLES F. STANLEY

"As for God, His way is blameless; the word of the LORD is tried;
He is a shield to all who take refuge in Him. For who is God,
but the LORD? And who is a rock, except our God, the God who
girds me with strength and makes my way blameless?"

—PSALM 18:30-32

The Bible is the written record of God's unfolding revelation of Himself—His ways, character, and nature—through the spoken word, in history, and ultimately through the coming of His Son, Jesus Christ, into the world.

DR. CHARLES F. STANLEY

 In the beginning was the Word, and the Word was with God, and the Word was God.

—JOHN 1:1

God's eternal Word is infallible,
inerrant, and everlasting—which
simply means it is without error.
Our God of truth would not
give us a book of mistakes
to be our guide.

DR. CHARLES F. STANLEY

All Scripture is inspired by God and profitable for
teaching, for reproof, for correction, for training
in righteousness; so that the man of God may be
adequate, equipped for every good work.

—2 TIMOTHY 3:16-17

God gives us enough light to follow
the paths He has for us. He's not
going to show us the entire way
from the beginning—just one step
at a time as we need it.

DR. CHARLES F. STANLEY

Trust in the LORD with all your heart and
do not lean on your own understanding.
In all your ways acknowledge Him, and He
will make your paths straight.

—PROVERBS 3:5-6

The awareness of God's presence energizes us for our work.

Jesus came up and spoke to them, saying, "All authority has been given to Me in heaven and on earth. Go therefore and make disciples of all the nations, baptizing them in the name of the Father and the Son and the Holy Spirit, teaching them to observe all that I commanded you; and lo, I am with you always, even to the end of the age."

—MATTHEW 28:18-20

We experience the presence
of God when He reveals Himself
to us by His Spirit. He does so
in order to enable, energize,
inform, strengthen, and warn
us—or simply to give us joy.

DR. CHARLES F. STANLEY

We have received, not the spirit of the world, but the Spirit who is from God, so that
we may know the things freely given to us by God, which things we also speak, not in
words taught by human wisdom, but in those taught by the Spirit, combining spiritual
thoughts with spiritual words. . . . He who is spiritual appraises all things, yet he
himself is appraised by no one. For WHO HAS KNOWN THE MIND OF THE LORD, THAT HE
WILL INSTRUCT HIM? But we have the mind of Christ.

—1 CORINTHIANS 2:12-13, 15-16

The Spirit of God does for us what we cannot do for ourselves. The Father has sent His Spirit to live the life of Christ in and through us because His ultimate goal is to conform us to His likeness.

DR. CHARLES F. STANLEY

Be renewed in the spirit of your mind, and put on the new self, which in the likeness of God has been created in righteousness and holiness of the truth.

—EPHESIANS 4:23-24

Despite the fact that He is the Sovereign of the universe—the Creator, Savior, Lord, and Master who rules and reigns— He has condescended to live in our lives, through the regeneration of the Holy Spirit, so we can communicate with Him.

DR. CHARLES F. STANLEY

O LORD, our Lord, how majestic is Your name in all the earth, who have displayed Your splendor above the heavens! . . . When I consider Your heavens, the work of Your fingers, the moon and the stars, which You have ordained; what is man that You take thought of him, and the son of man that You care for him? Yet You have made him a little lower than God, and You crown him with glory and majesty!

—PSALM 8:1, 3-5

It is awesome what happens
when you are aware of God's
presence in your life. There is no
limitation to what you can do as
long as it is within His will.

DR. CHARLES F. STANLEY

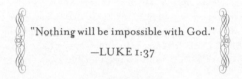

"Nothing will be impossible with God."
—LUKE 1:37

Don't degrade or devalue yourself because of events in your past. God has something important for you to do. He is interested in working in your life.

DR. CHARLES F. STANLEY

Christ Jesus came into the world to save sinners, among whom I am foremost of all. Yet for this reason I found mercy, so that in me as the foremost, Jesus Christ might demonstrate His perfect patience as an example for those who would believe in Him for eternal life. Now to the King eternal, immortal, invisible, the only God, be honor and glory forever and ever. Amen.

—I TIMOTHY 1:15-17

God doesn't make mistakes, and
He doesn't do anything without
a purpose. When He speaks to
your spirit, revealing Himself to
you, He has something awesome
in mind—and He wants to know if
you're willing to listen.

DR. CHARLES F. STANLEY

"The eyes of the LORD move to and fro throughout the earth that He
may strongly support those whose heart is completely His."
— 2 CHRONICLES 16:9

God does not require us to understand His will, just obey it, even if it seems unreasonable.

When He had finished speaking, He said to Simon, "Put out into the deep water and let down your nets for a catch." Simon answered and said, "Master, we worked hard all night and caught nothing, but I will do as You say and let down the nets." When they had done this, they enclosed a great quantity of fish, and their nets began to break.

—LUKE 5:4-6

God has a plan for your life, and
He's with you in that plan.
It would be out of character
for the Father to call you to do
something then not help you
accomplish it. He always
gets involved.

DR. CHARLES F. STANLEY

 Now the God of peace, who brought up from the dead the great
Shepherd of the sheep through the blood of the eternal covenant,
even Jesus our Lord, equip you in every good thing to do His will,
working in us that which is pleasing in His sight, through Jesus
Christ, to whom be the glory forever and ever. Amen.

—HEBREWS 13:20-21

God is going to require you to do things that do not seem reasonable. What you have to decide is, *Am I going to obey the Lord, even when things don't look reasonable to me?* Remember, common sense is not enough to judge your situation. You need God's omniscience—His knowledge, wisdom, and full understanding.

DR. CHARLES F. STANLEY

"My thoughts are not your thoughts, nor are your ways My ways," declares the LORD. "For as the heavens are higher than the earth, so are My ways higher than your ways and My thoughts than your thoughts."

—ISAIAH 55:8-9

Throughout the years, whenever God has said "No" to me, He's been right every single time. Why? Simply because He's obligated by His holy character and unfailing love to give you and I the absolute best direction for our lives.

DR. CHARLES F. STANLEY

The law of the LORD is perfect, restoring the soul; the testimony of the LORD is sure, making wise the simple. The precepts of the LORD are right, rejoicing the heart; the commandment of the LORD is pure, enlightening the eyes. The fear of the LORD is clean, enduring forever; the judgments of the LORD are true; they are righteous altogether. . . . By them Your servant is warned; in keeping them there is great reward.

—PSALM 19:7-9, 11

Everything you are concerned about or that causes you to hesitate, God has already figured it out. Before He called you, He knew how to solve every challenge you would ever encounter.

DR. CHARLES F. STANLEY

God is able to make all grace abound to you, so that always having all sufficiency in everything, you may have an abundance for every good deed.

—2 CORINTHIANS 9:8

You are a creation of God, made for the purpose of bringing Him glory and honor. The best, most effective thing you can do is walk in the center of His will.

DR. CHARLES F. STANLEY

"Worthy are You, our Lord and our God, to receive glory and honor and power; for You created all things, and because of Your will they existed, and were created."

—REVELATION 4:11

God's plan for your life has incredible blessings and unexpected rewards. Following Him will not only be profitable for you, but it will also allow you to glimpse Jesus—His trustworthiness, willingness to forgive your sins, faithfulness, loyalty, devotion, and His unconditional love for you.

DR. CHARLES F. STANLEY

See how great a love the Father has bestowed on us, that we would be called children of God; and such we are.

—1 JOHN 3:1

You reap what you sow,
more than you sow, and
later than you sow.

Do not be deceived, God is not mocked; for whatever a man sows,
this he will also reap. For the one who sows to his own flesh will
from the flesh reap corruption, but the one who sows to the Spirit
will from the Spirit reap eternal life. Let us not lose heart in doing
good, for in due time we will reap if we do not grow weary.
So then, while we have opportunity, let us do good to all people,
and especially to those who are of the household of the faith.

—GALATIANS 6:7-10

Life is full of choices, and those we make early on remain with us for the rest of our lives. All we see, hear, and experience as children are seeds that eventually influence our characters.

DR. CHARLES F. STANLEY

 Train up a child in the way he should go, even when he is old he will not depart from it.

—PROVERBS 22:6

Do not allow yourself to be misled by thinking that you can sin, rebel against God, and get away with it. That's deception. It does not happen.

DR. CHARLES F. STANLEY

Each one is tempted when he is carried away and enticed by his own lust. Then when lust has conceived, it gives birth to sin; and when sin is accomplished, it brings forth death. Do not be deceived, my beloved brethren.

—JAMES 1:14-16

If I am sowing something, that means I am craving it—absorbing it and accepting it into my life. Why do people look at and do sinful things? Simply because they are feeding their desires to be independent of God. But you cannot feed on things without experiencing their consequences.

DR. CHARLES F. STANLEY

 They sow the wind and they reap the whirlwind.

—HOSEA 8:7

You can either sow to the flesh, or you can sow to the Spirit. When you read the Word of God, you are planting it in your mind and heart. You are sowing to the Spirit. When you share your testimony, attend church, and write down godly truths, the influence and impact of the Spirit of God are growing in your life.

DR. CHARLES F. STANLEY

The fruit of the Spirit is love, joy, peace, patience, kindness, goodness, faithfulness, gentleness, self-control; against such things there is no law.

—GALATIANS 5:22-23

You can do many things for people
that do not result in lasting fruit.
But when you share with others the
truth of Jesus—praying for them
and talking to them about what the
Lord has done in your life—God
will use you to reap great, eternal
harvests in them.

DR. CHARLES F. STANLEY

 "The harvest is plentiful, but the workers are
few. Therefore beseech the Lord of the harvest
to send out workers into His harvest."

—MATTHEW 9:37-38

Eternal life has two qualities—
the *length* of time and the *quality*
of life. When we sow seeds that
are righteous, holy, and godly,
we are building eternal value
into our lives. We are going to
become stronger and godlier in
our conduct and thinking, and
our lives will also have greater
influence on those around us.

DR. CHARLES F. STANLEY

"Those who have insight will shine brightly like the
brightness of the expanse of heaven, and those who lead the
many to righteousness, like the stars forever and ever."

—DANIEL 12:3

7

The dark moments of our lives will last only so long as is necessary for God to accomplish His purpose in us.

"Do not be grieved or angry with yourselves, because you sold me here . . . . God sent me before you to preserve for you a remnant in the earth, and to keep you alive by a great deliverance. Now, therefore, it was not you who sent me here, but God; and He has made me a father to Pharaoh and lord of all his household and ruler over all the land of Egypt."

—GENESIS 45:5, 7–8

If you desire God's best in your life and want to make your life count, then you can expect to travel the road of adversity.

DR. CHARLES F. STANLEY

Although the Lord has given you bread of privation and water of oppression, He, your Teacher will no longer hide Himself, but your eyes will behold your Teacher. Your ears will hear a word behind you, "This is the way, walk in it," whenever you turn to the right or to the left.

—ISAIAH 30:20-21

There are some moments in life that are absolutely midnight black. With very little hope, you see no way God could possibly deliver you from them. But take comfort—the Father has a plan for you in these times, and He allows them for a purpose.

DR. CHARLES F. STANLEY

We were burdened excessively, beyond our strength, so that we despaired even of life; indeed, we had the sentence of death within ourselves so that we would not trust in ourselves, but in God who raises the dead; who delivered us from so great a peril of death, and will deliver us, He on whom we have set our hope.

—2 CORINTHIANS 1:8-10

God teaches us discipline—we do what He instructs, whether we understand or not. He teaches us perseverance—we keep going and don't give up. He also teaches us He is in charge of our lives, no matter what happens. Regardless of our circumstances, we come to understand God is still God.

DR. CHARLES F. STANLEY

"Shall we indeed accept good from God
and not accept adversity?"

—JOB 2:10

God's ultimate purpose in our lives—the reason He uses dark moments—is to conform us to the likeness of Jesus so our characters become like Christ's.

DR. CHARLES F. STANLEY

 If we have become united with Him in the likeness of His death, certainly we shall also be in the likeness of His resurrection.

—ROMANS 6:5

God is leading us to surrender, showing us what it means to live a yielded life. He is bringing us to the point where we can say, "God, I don't like this difficulty. I don't understand it, but I'm willing to trust You no matter what."

DR. CHARLES F. STANLEY

 "Who is among you that fears the LORD, that obeys the voice of His servant, that walks in darkness and has no light? Let him trust in the name of the LORD and rely on his God."

—ISAIAH 50:10

God puts limitations on your trials,
dark moments, and temptations.
Whatever you're facing—whether it
involves your health, relationships,
finances, or whatever it might be—
it will not go on forever. The Father
is teaching you to trust Him and
persevere. He seeks to make you
courageous, bold, trustworthy, faithful,
diligent, and disciplined. These are
God's purposes ... but you must
yield to Him.

DR. CHARLES F. STANLEY

The Lord will not reject forever, for if He causes
grief, then He will have compassion according to
His abundant lovingkindness. For He does not
afflict willingly or grieve the sons of men.

—LAMENTATIONS 3:31-33

Fight all your battles on your knees, and you win every time.

*Jesus came with them to a place called Gethsemane, and said
to His disciples, "Sit here while I go over there and pray."
. . . He went a little beyond them, and fell on His face and
prayed, saying, "My Father, if it is possible, let this cup pass
from Me; yet not as I will, but as You will."*

—MATTHEW 26:36, 39

The one thing Satan does not want you to do is pray. If he can keep you busy, anxious, and distracted enough—if he can keep you off your knees and away from God—then he doesn't care what else you do.

DR. CHARLES F. STANLEY

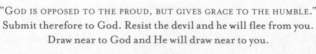

"GOD IS OPPOSED TO THE PROUD, BUT GIVES GRACE TO THE HUMBLE."
Submit therefore to God. Resist the devil and he will flee from you.
Draw near to God and He will draw near to you.

—JAMES 4:6–8

The most important thing in your
life is your personal, intimate
relationship with the Father.
For it to be right, you must
have the right kind of prayer life.

DR. CHARLES F. STANLEY

My prayer is to You, O LORD, at an acceptable
time; O God, in the greatness of Your lovingkindness,
answer me with Your saving truth.

—PSALM 69:13

Fighting our battles on our knees means that we go before Holy God in reverence for who He is, placing our petitions, fears, wars, and struggles before the Sovereign of the universe and entrusting them to His care.

DR. CHARLES F. STANLEY

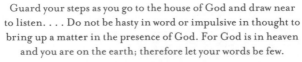

Guard your steps as you go to the house of God and draw near to listen. . . . Do not be hasty in word or impulsive in thought to bring up a matter in the presence of God. For God is in heaven and you are on the earth; therefore let your words be few.

—ECCLESIASTES 5:1-2

Engage God. Bring Him into your battle so you're not fighting alone. He is absolutely omnipotent—He has all power. He is absolutely omniscient—He has all knowledge. He is omnipresent—He is always with you. He will not fail you in the battle.

DR. CHARLES F. STANLEY

 "Be strong and courageous, do not fear or be dismayed . . . for the one with us is greater than the one with him. With him is only an arm of flesh, but with us is the LORD our God to help us and to fight our battles."

—2 CHRONICLES 32:7-8

You get the greatest amount of comfort, assurance, and confidence when you spend time alone with God. He speaks to you and encourages your heart. He lifts you up and shares His viewpoint, letting you know— from His perspective—what you should do next.

DR. CHARLES F. STANLEY

 You will make known to me the path of life; in Your presence is fullness of joy; in Your right hand there are pleasures forever.

—PSALM 16:11

One of the keys to victory in any situation is to see everything that happens to you or is said to you as coming from God, rather than from the person who says or does it.

DR. CHARLES F. STANLEY

If someone says, "I love God," and hates his brother, he is a liar; for the one who does not love his brother whom he has seen, cannot love God whom he has not seen.

—1 JOHN 4:20

Trusting God means looking beyond what we can see to what God sees.

David said to the Philistine, "You come to me with a sword, a spear, and a javelin, but I come to you in the name of the LORD of hosts, the God of the armies of Israel, whom you have taunted. This day the LORD will deliver you up into my hands . . . that all the earth may know that there is a God in Israel, and that all this assembly may know that the LORD does not deliver by sword or by spear; for the battle is the LORD'S and He will give you into our hands."

—1 SAMUEL 17:45-47

Faith is at the heart of everything we believe and everything we are in the Christian life.

DR. CHARLES F. STANLEY

 Faith is the assurance of things hoped for, the conviction of things not seen.

—HEBREWS 11:1

God is willing to give you the capacity to see what the human eye cannot see. When there is no evidence and no reason to believe His promise will be fulfilled, the Father gives you the ability to see it finished, completed, and done.

DR. CHARLES F. STANLEY

 Who is the man who fears the LORD? He will instruct him in the way he should choose. . . . The secret of the LORD is for those who fear Him, and He will make them know His covenant.

—PSALM 25:12, 14

If you want God to maximize the impact of your life and grant you peace, you have to completely trust Him. If you live your life trusting Him, you're not fretting. You're not worried. And what happens? You're able to obey Him fully.

DR. CHARLES F. STANLEY

Do not fret because of evildoers, be not envious toward wrongdoers. For they will wither quickly like the grass and fade like the green herb. Trust in the LORD and do good; dwell in the land and cultivate faithfulness. Delight yourself in the LORD; and He will give you the desires of your heart. Commit your way to the LORD, trust also in Him, and He will do it. He will bring forth your righteousness as the light and your judgment as the noonday.

—PSALM 37:1-6

If you're making a mistake about
what you're asking of God, He will
show you what that mistake is, and
He will help you straighten it out.

DR. CHARLES F. STANLEY

 The steps of a man are established by the LORD, and He
delights in his way, When he falls, he will not be hurled
headlong, because the LORD is the One who holds his hand.

—PSALM 37:23-24

God doesn't keep secrets. He wants you to know the truth about what is going on in your life. If you are genuinely seeking to know His will, He is going to show you what you need to know.

DR. CHARLES F. STANLEY

"It is He who reveals the profound and hidden things; He knows what is in the darkness, and the light dwells with Him. To You, O God of my fathers, I give thanks and praise, for You have given me wisdom and power; even now You have made known to me what we requested of You."

—DANIEL 2:22-23

God doesn't have favorites.
He has intimates—those who are
willing to walk in His will and
rely upon Him to show the way.
This requires trust, faith, and
complete surrender.

DR. CHARLES F. STANLEY

"As for you, my son Solomon, know the God of your father,
and serve Him with a whole heart and a willing mind; for the
LORD searches all hearts, and understands every intent of the
thoughts. If you seek Him, He will let you find Him."

—1 CHRONICLES 28:9

If necessary, God will move heaven and earth to show us His will.

"I know the plans that I have for you," declares the LORD,
"plans for welfare and not for calamity to give you a future
and a hope. Then you will call upon Me and come and pray
to Me, and I will listen to you. You will seek Me and find Me
when you search for Me with all your heart."

—JEREMIAH 29:11-13

God loves you just the way you are
and wants to enable you to become
everything He created you to be.
He has a purpose and plan for
your life and is more than willing
to show you exactly how He wants
to use you for His glory.

DR. CHARLES F. STANLEY

 My frame was not hidden from You, when I was made in secret, and
skillfully wrought in the depths of the earth; Your eyes have seen my
unformed substance; and in Your book were all written the days that
were ordained for me, when as yet there was not one of them.

—PSALM 139:15-16

If you neglect the Word of God, you're going to step out of the will of God.

DR. CHARLES F. STANLEY

How blessed are those whose way is blameless, who walk in the law of the LORD. How blessed are those who observe His testimonies, who seek Him with all their heart. They also do no unrighteousness; they walk in His ways.

—PSALM 119:1-3

If you are praying, reading the Word of God, and still not getting anywhere, then examine your heart. Look at what is going on inside of you. God will not withhold the truth—He is always willing to speak to you.

DR. CHARLES F. STANLEY

Thus the Lord GOD, the Holy One of Israel, has said, "In repentance and rest you will be saved, in quietness and trust is your strength." But you were not willing. . . . . Therefore the LORD longs to be gracious to you, and therefore He waits on high to have compassion on you. For the LORD is a God of justice; how blessed are all those who long for Him.

—ISAIAH 30:15, 18

How long must you wait for the Father to reveal His will to you? As long as is necessary to spiritually prepare you for what He has to tell you. It all depends upon your willingness to listen to Him and the timing for His perfect plan to be accomplished.

DR. CHARLES F. STANLEY

 I trust in You, O Lord, I say, "You are my God." My times are in Your hand; deliver me from the hand of my enemies and from those who persecute me. Make Your face to shine upon Your servant; save me in Your lovingkindness.

—PSALM 31:14-16

The walk of faith is taken one step at a time.

DR. CHARLES F. STANLEY

Without faith it is impossible to please Him, for he
who comes to God must believe that He is and that
He is a rewarder of those who seek Him.

—HEBREWS 11:6

You invest your time
based on how much you
value someone or something,
and nothing is more valuable than
your intimate relationship with
God. If you are too busy to pray
or wait for Him to reveal
His will to you, then you are
headed for trouble.

DR. CHARLES F. STANLEY

Our soul waits for the LORD; He is our help and our shield.
For our heart rejoices in Him, because we trust in His
holy name. Let Your lovingkindness, O LORD, be upon us,
according as we have hoped in You.

—PSALM 33:20-22

God assumes full responsibility for our needs when we obey Him.

*My God will supply all your needs according
to His riches in glory in Christ Jesus.*
—PHILIPPIANS 4:19

Any time you give with the
right heart and spirit, God is
going to bless you.

DR. CHARLES F. STANLEY

"You shall generously give to him, and your heart
shall not be grieved when you give to him, because
for this thing the LORD your God will bless you in
all your work and in all your undertakings."

—DEUTERONOMY 15:10

On what basis do I ask the
Father to meet a particular need
in my life? Simply this—He
promised He would do so.

DR. CHARLES F. STANLEY

"Ask, and it will be given to you; seek, and you
will find; knock, and it will be opened to you. For
everyone who asks receives, and he who seeks finds,
and to him who knocks it will be opened."

—MATTHEW 7:7-8

The God whom we serve and
love not only has the ability to
meet every need we have, but He
also has the integrity to keep His
promises to us.

DR. CHARLES F. STANLEY

The LORD God is a sun and shield; the LORD gives
grace and glory; no good thing does He
withhold from those who walk uprightly.

—PSALM 84:11

God is our awesome, wonderful, loving Father. He wants us to align our thinking with His—to get us to the point where we ask Him to provide for us on His schedule and through the channel He chooses, understanding that the limitations we place on Him only hinder His will being accomplished in our lives.

DR. CHARLES F. STANLEY

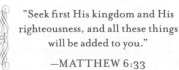

"Seek first His kingdom and His righteousness, and all these things will be added to you."

—MATTHEW 6:33

Don't focus on the need.
Focus on the Father.

DR. CHARLES F. STANLEY

Though the fig tree should not blossom and there be no fruit on the vines, though the yield of the olive should fail and the fields produce no food, though the flock should be cut off from the fold and there be no cattle in the stalls, yet I will exult in the LORD, I will rejoice in the God of my salvation. The Lord GOD is my strength, and He has made my feet like hinds' feet, and makes me walk on my high places.

—HABAKKUK 3:17-19

What does it mean to trust God?
It means I ask Him for what I
need, believe He has heard me,
thank Him when He confirms
He will fulfill His promise to me,
and then I walk with the
assurance in my heart that He
will meet my need.

DR. CHARLES F. STANLEY

"All things for which you pray and ask,
believe that you have received them,
and they will be granted you."

—MARK 11:24

Peace with God is the fruit of oneness with God.

"Do not let your heart be troubled; believe in God,
believe also in Me. . . . Peace I leave with you; My peace
I give to you; not as the world gives do I give to you. Do
not let your heart be troubled, nor let it be fearful."

—JOHN 14:1, 27

Can you have peace during difficult, trying times when your circumstances seem unmanageable, and you don't have any idea what is going to happen? Yes you can. You can experience a tranquility that is so profound and reassuring, it endures deep within, despite whatever happens. It is based on the security you have with God—the only One who can truly give you unshakable peace.

DR. CHARLES F. STANLEY

You have put gladness in my heart, more than when their grain and new wine abound. In peace I will both lie down and sleep, for You alone, O LORD, make me to dwell in safety.

—PSALM 4:7-8

The first step to having the peace *of* God in your life is to make peace *with* God.

DR. CHARLES F. STANLEY

Having been justified by faith, we have peace with God through our Lord Jesus Christ, through whom also we have obtained our introduction by faith into this grace in which we stand; and we exult in hope of the glory of God.

—ROMANS 5:1-2

In Greek, the word *peace* means
"to bind together." Jesus binds us
to Himself, bringing us into
oneness with the Father. You are
in agreement with Him—and
where there is agreement and
unity, there is peace.

DR. CHARLES F. STANLEY

"The glory which You have given Me I have given to them, that
they may be one, just as We are one; I in them and You in Me,
that they may be perfected in unity, so that the world may know
that You sent Me, and loved them, even as You have loved Me."

—JOHN 17:22-23

Everything you and I desire to be—the characteristics that make us like our Savior—the Spirit of God produces all of those essential traits within us. So what is our responsibility? Our responsibility is to remain one with Him.

DR. CHARLES F. STANLEY

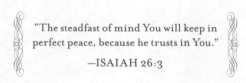

"The steadfast of mind You will keep in perfect peace, because he trusts in You."

—ISAIAH 26:3

People try to find peace in
all sorts of things. They think,
*If I could just be married or have more sex,
I'd have peace,* or, *If I could just own this
or that, I could have peace. If I were more
beautiful or handsome, if I had more wealth,
or if I took a couple of drinks, then I would
feel better.* But none of those things
guarantees any peace whatsoever. Why?
All are fleeting—they change. There's
nothing solid or eternal about them, and
the result is consternation and confusion.

DR. CHARLES F. STANLEY

 "Peace, peace to him who is far and to him who is near,"
says the LORD, "and I will heal him." But the wicked are
like the tossing sea, for it cannot be quiet.

—ISAIAH 57:19-20

Jesus is your peace, no matter what comes your way. Regardless of your circumstances, there is a tranquility, serenity, and calmness that anchors your soul. You're not blown about by the winds of adversity and heartache. The Lord stabilizes you by His awesome promises and by who He is within you.

DR. CHARLES F. STANLEY

 "These things I have spoken to you, so that in Me you may have peace. In the world you have tribulation, but take courage; I have overcome the world."

—JOHN 16:33

Listening to God is essential to walking with God.

Prove yourselves doers of the word, and not merely hearers who delude themselves. For if anyone is a hearer of the word and not a doer, he is like a man who looks at his natural face in a mirror; for once he has looked at himself and gone away, he has immediately forgotten what kind of person he was. But one who looks intently at the perfect law, the law of liberty, and abides by it, not having become a forgetful hearer but an effectual doer, this man will be blessed in what he does.

—JAMES 1:22–25

God's will is for every one of us to walk with Him. But in order for you and I to stay in the center of His will, we must learn a very valuable lesson—we must learn to listen to Him.

DR. CHARLES F. STANLEY

"The LORD will surely bless you in the land which the LORD your God is giving you as an inheritance to possess, if only you listen obediently to the voice of the LORD your God, to observe carefully all this commandment which I am commanding you today. For the LORD your God will bless you as He has promised you."

—DEUTERONOMY 15:4-6

Purposeful listeners pay close attention to what the Father is teaching them in order to learn, absorb, and incorporate the truth they've heard into their lives.

DR. CHARLES F. STANLEY

"Everyone who hears these words of Mine and acts on them, may be compared to a wise man who built his house on the rock. And the rain fell, and the floods came, and the winds blew and slammed against that house; and yet it did not fall, for it had been founded on the rock."

—MATTHEW 7:24-25

The Christian life is
serious business. You cannot
live it apart from the work
of the Holy Spirit.

DR. CHARLES F. STANLEY

"The Helper, the Holy Spirit, whom the Father will
send in My name, He will teach you all things, and bring
to your remembrance all that I said to you."

—JOHN 14:26

It is fine to read through the Bible in one year—in fact, it is a wonderful goal. However, it is much more important to read a portion of Scripture every day and listen for God to speak to you, giving you instruction through it.

DR. CHARLES F. STANLEY

"This book of the law shall not depart from your mouth, but you shall meditate on it day and night, so that you may be careful to do according to all that is written in it; for then you will make your way prosperous, and then you will have success."

—JOSHUA 1:8

God never speaks in a way that
contradicts His Word.

DR. CHARLES F. STANLEY

"The Glory of Israel will not lie or change
His mind; for He is not a man that He
should change His mind."

— I SAMUEL 15:29

The Sovereign of the universe has all power to meet every single need you have, to answer your prayers, and to give you direction. He's willing to speak if you're willing to listen.

DR. CHARLES F. STANLEY

"Listen to My voice, and do according to all which I command you; so you shall be My people, and I will be your God."

—JEREMIAH 11:4

God acts on behalf of those who wait for Him.

You did awesome things which we did not expect, You came down, the mountains quaked at Your presence. For from days of old they have not heard or perceived by ear, nor has the eye seen a God besides You, who acts in behalf of the one who waits for Him.

—ISAIAH 64:3-4

God created everything with a plan, and He has principles that govern all He does. The Lord always operates with a sense of direction and purpose in mind— not only for us as individuals, but also to achieve His universal, eternal goals.

DR. CHARLES F. STANLEY

O LORD, You are my God; I will exalt You, I will give thanks to Your name; for You have worked wonders, plans formed long ago, with perfect faithfulness.

—ISAIAH 25:1

Throughout our lives, the Father encourages us along the way. He protects us—safeguarding the outcome of our obedience to Him. He shields us from situations and circumstances we're not even aware of. He heals, comforts, and teaches us. He answers our prayers. He is a very personal God—He is intimately involved in every detail of our lives.

DR. CHARLES F. STANLEY

"As for God, His way is blameless; the word of the LORD is tested; He is a shield to all who take refuge in Him. For who is God, besides the LORD? And who is a rock, besides our God? God is my strong fortress; and He sets the blameless in His way. He makes my feet like hinds' feet, and sets me on my high places. He trains my hands for battle, so that my arms can bend a bow of bronze. You have also given me the shield of Your salvation, and Your help makes me great. You enlarge my steps under me, and my feet have not slipped."
—2 SAMUEL 22:31-37

What does it mean to wait upon God? When He has not answered your petition, granted your request, or when you do not see anything happening, what does it mean to be patient with Him? It means you are willing to wait—you are prepared to pause until He gives you further instruction on how to proceed.

DR. CHARLES F. STANLEY

The Everlasting God, the LORD, the Creator of the ends of the earth does not become weary or tired. His understanding is inscrutable. He gives strength to the weary, and to him who lacks might He increases power. Though youths grow weary and tired, and vigorous young men stumble badly, yet those who wait for the LORD will gain new strength; they will mount up with wings like eagles, they will run and not get tired, they will walk and not become weary.

—ISAIAH 40:28-31

Patience takes courage and humility. It means I am willing to lay aside my gratification. I am willing to wait for His intervention. I am willing to remove all the deadlines and trust God to act.

DR. CHARLES F. STANLEY

I would have despaired unless I had believed that I would see the goodness of the LORD in the land of the living. Wait for the LORD; be strong and let your heart take courage; yes, wait for the LORD.

—PSALM 27:13-14

Mark it down: When you're waiting for God's timing, you're waiting for His very best.

DR. CHARLES F. STANLEY

 My soul, wait in silence for God only, for my hope is from Him. He only is my rock and my salvation, my stronghold; I shall not be shaken. On God my salvation and my glory rest; the rock of my strength, my refuge is in God. Trust in Him at all times, O people; pour out your heart before Him; God is a refuge for us.

—PSALM 62:5-8

We make the greatest impact
in our Christian lives when we
choose to wait upon the Lord.
This is our testimony of the
reality of God to the people
around us. By watching our
steadfast faith in Him, they learn
He is truly trustworthy.

DR. CHARLES F. STANLEY

I waited patiently for the LORD; and He inclined to me and
heard my cry. He brought me up out of the pit of destruction,
out of the miry clay, and He set my feet upon a rock making my
footsteps firm. He put a new song in my mouth, a song of praise
to our God; many will see and fear and will trust in the LORD.

—PSALM 40:1-3

Brokenness is God's requirement for maximum usefulness.

He has said to me, "My grace is sufficient for you, for power is perfected in weakness." Most gladly, therefore, I will rather boast about my weaknesses, so that the power of Christ may dwell in me. Therefore I am well content with weaknesses, with insults, with distresses, with persecutions, with difficulties, for Christ's sake; for when I am weak, then I am strong.

—2 CORINTHIANS 12:9–10

We crush grapes to create wine.
We grind wheat to make bread. And
God breaks our self-will to make us
useful vessels for His kingdom.

DR. CHARLES F. STANLEY

 "Behold, I have refined you, but not as silver;
I have tested you in the furnace of affliction.
For My own sake, for My own sake, I will act."

—ISAIAH 48:10-11

What is brokenness? It is God's method for dealing with our self-lives—the desire within us to act independently of Him. He has purposed to bring every area of our lives into submission, so He will continue to remove every obstacle until we fully trust Him and completely surrender ourselves to Him.

DR. CHARLES F. STANLEY

 All discipline for the moment seems not to be joyful, but sorrowful; yet to those who have been trained by it, afterwards it yields the peaceful fruit of righteousness. —HEBREWS 12:11

God wants you to be useful for His kingdom. There is no such thing as an insignificant person to Him. You're important in God's eyes, and He has an incredible plan for your life.

DR. CHARLES F. STANLEY

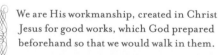

We are His workmanship, created in Christ Jesus for good works, which God prepared beforehand so that we would walk in them.

—EPHESIANS 2:10

God will work through you to
the degree in which you allow
yourself to be brought into
harmony with His will, purpose,
and plan for your life.

DR. CHARLES F. STANLEY

 "I am the vine, you are the branches; he who
abides in Me and I in him, he bears much fruit,
for apart from Me you can do nothing."

—JOHN 15:5

God isn't interested in eloquence
or skill. He is interested in
a surrendered life, yielded to Him
for the purpose of bringing
Him glory. So you must ask yourself
this question: *Am I living
for Him, or am I living for myself?*

DR. CHARLES F. STANLEY

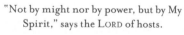

"Not by might nor by power, but by My
Spirit," says the LORD of hosts.

—ZECHARIAH 4:6

I don't know of anyone in life more miserable than the Christian who refuses to be broken. To have talents, skills, abilities, experiences, and looks—you name it—but to be on the shelf, unused by God, is wretched. The brokenness of God is an act of love for you from your heavenly Father. Don't resist it.

DR. CHARLES F. STANLEY

It is for discipline that you endure; God deals with you as with sons; for what son is there whom his father does not discipline? . . . We had earthly fathers to discipline us, and we respected them; shall we not much rather be subject to the Father of spirits, and live?

—HEBREWS 12:7, 9

Whatever you acquire outside of God's will eventually turns to ashes.

"The son said to him, 'Father, I have sinned against heaven and in your sight; I am no longer worthy to be called your son.' But the father said to his slaves, 'Quickly bring out the best robe and put it on him, and put a ring on his hand and sandals on his feet; and bring the fattened calf, kill it, and let us eat and celebrate; for this son of mine was dead and has come to life again; he was lost and has been found.' And they began to celebrate."

—LUKE 15:21-24

When you pursue things that are outside the will of God, you will be disappointed and disillusioned. Before long, you will find yourself discouraged with life. But the Father has fixed it so that if you will seek His will and trust Him, He will give you His very best. Then you will understand what true peace, contentment, and joy are all about.

DR. CHARLES F. STANLEY

Thus says the LORD, "Let not a wise man boast of his wisdom, and let not the mighty man boast of his might, let not a rich man boast of his riches; but let him who boasts boast of this, that he understands and knows Me, that I am the LORD who exercises lovingkindness, justice and righteousness on earth; for I delight in these things," declares the LORD.

—JEREMIAH 9:23-24

There are some folks who have made ungodly choices but seem to be doing fantastic in life. However, what you and I can't see is the pain they face on the inside. There are also many people who have a great deal—wealth, social status, power—but who are utterly miserable. On the other hand, there are many people who have very little who are genuinely happy. Why? They have an intimate relationship with Almighty God.

DR. CHARLES F. STANLEY

Do not let your heart envy sinners, but live in the fear of the LORD always. Surely there is a future, and your hope will not be cut off.

—PROVERBS 23:17-18

Like the prodigal son, we
find ourselves in a far country
anywhere, anytime you and
I live outside the will
of God. It is dangerous,
impoverishing territory.

DR. CHARLES F. STANLEY

"The younger son gathered everything together and went on a journey into
a distant country, and there he squandered his estate with loose living. Now
when he had spent everything, a severe famine occurred in that country, and
he began to be impoverished. . . . When he came to his senses, he said, 'How
many of my father's hired men have more than enough bread, but I am dying
here with hunger! I will get up and go to my father.'"

—LUKE 15:13-14, 17-18

Spiritually, ashes are the remains
of disobedience, rebellion, lust,
and all of the sins that distract you
from the will of God. All you are
left with is guilt, regret, shame,
and emptiness.

DR. CHARLES F. STANLEY

The wages of sin is death, but
the free gift of God is eternal life
in Christ Jesus our Lord.

—ROMANS 6:23

Wouldn't it be something if God gave us a 60-second glimpse of the last year of our lives? We probably couldn't stand it. All the churches would be full. People would be saved and recommitting themselves to the Lord by the millions because suddenly they would know the truth and see things as God sees them.

DR. CHARLES F. STANLEY

We will all stand before the judgment seat of God. For it is written,
"As I live, says the Lord, every knee shall bow to Me,
and every tongue shall give praise to God." So then each one
of us will give an account of himself to God.

—ROMANS 14:10-12

Sin has penalties and leaves scars.
Often, it costs us things we will
never recover. But the forgiveness
of God is ours for the asking.

DR. CHARLES F. STANLEY

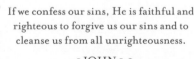

If we confess our sins, He is faithful and
righteous to forgive us our sins and to
cleanse us from all unrighteousness.

—1 JOHN 1:9

We stand tallest and strongest on our knees.

"O Lord, I beseech You, may Your ear be attentive to the prayer of Your servant and the prayer of Your servants who delight to revere Your name, and make Your servant successful today and grant him compassion."

—NEHEMIAH 1:11

Prayer is the choice tool God has given us to reach Him, speak to Him, plead our case before Him, and receive all we need from Him. Unfortunately, we take prayer—one of the greatest blessings He has given us—for granted.

DR. CHARLES F. STANLEY

Let everyone who is godly pray to You in a time when You may be found; surely in a flood of great waters they will not reach him. You are my hiding place; You preserve me from trouble; You surround me with songs of deliverance.

—PSALM 32:6-7

Kneeling before God isn't just how you approach Him physically. In fact, there are many people who cannot kneel for one reason or another. Rather, it is an attitude of the heart in which you recognize Him as the Sovereign of this universe. You don't just hope He will answer your prayers, you trust, believe, and expect Him to help you.

DR. CHARLES F. STANLEY

"I am God, and there is no other. I have sworn by Myself, the word has gone forth from My mouth in righteousness and will not turn back, that to Me every knee will bow, every tongue will swear allegiance. They will say of Me, 'Only in the LORD are righteousness and strength.'"

—ISAIAH 45:22-24

Your prayers won't be answered
as long as you're holding
onto things that are sinful
in the eyes of God.

DR. CHARLES F. STANLEY

 Therefore, confess your sins to one another, and pray
for one another so that you may be healed. The effective
prayer of a righteous man can accomplish much.

—JAMES 5:16

If you want the power of God in your life, you must seek to be pure and holy in how you live and treat others. Purity of heart and the power of God are inextricably linked. This doesn't mean that you never make a mistake or go astray but that you are sensitive to sin and deal with it right away.

DR. CHARLES F. STANLEY

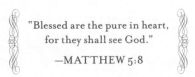

"Blessed are the pure in heart, for they shall see God."

—MATTHEW 5:8

When God calls you, He is not looking for information on what needs to be done or how difficult the task is. He already knows exactly what to do in every situation. He created you. He gave you abilities, talents, and skills. And He knows exactly how to help you accomplish His will through His power and strength.

DR. CHARLES F. STANLEY

"O LORD, the God of our fathers, are You not God in the heavens? And are You not ruler over all the kingdoms of the nations? Power and might are in Your hand so that no one can stand against You. . . . O our God . . . we are powerless before this great multitude who are coming against us; nor do we know what to do, but our eyes are on You."

—2 CHRONICLES 20:6, 12

It's not a sin to feel inadequate when thinking about the things God may require of us. Feeling inadequate is a part of recognizing our dependence upon Him—upon His awesome power, wisdom, love, and holiness.

DR. CHARLES F. STANLEY

 The LORD is my strength and my shield; my heart trusts in Him, and I am helped; therefore my heart exults, and with my song I shall thank Him.

—PSALM 28:7

As children of a
sovereign God, we are
never victims of our
circumstances.

*We know that God causes all things to work
together for good to those who love God, to those
who are called according to His purpose.*

—ROMANS 8:28

There are situations and circumstances so difficult and overwhelming, we don't know what to ask of the Father. But God loves us so much that He even helps us to pray. The Spirit of God, who is within us, knows our hearts and intercedes on our behalf.

DR. CHARLES F. STANLEY

He who searches the hearts knows what the mind of the Spirit is, because He intercedes for the saints according to the will of God.

—ROMANS 8:27

Do you really believe God is in absolute control of everything, or do you think He just rules over some things? What you believe about the Lord's power and authority in this world will affect how you view your circumstances.

DR. CHARLES F. STANLEY

The Lord is high above all nations; His glory is above the heavens. Who is like the Lord our God, who is enthroned on high, who humbles Himself to behold the things that are in heaven and in the earth? He raises the poor from the dust and lifts the needy from the ash heap.

—PSALM 113:4-7

God sees your future. He knows the end from the beginning and understands exactly what you need. He also knows precisely what it takes to form you into the person He created you to be.

DR. CHARLES F. STANLEY

"I am God, and there is no one like Me, declaring the end from the beginning, and from ancient times things which have not been done, saying, 'My purpose will be established, and I will accomplish all My good pleasure' . . . Truly I have spoken; truly I will bring it to pass. I have planned it, surely I will do it."

—ISAIAH 46:9-11

The conclusive truth is that
all of our circumstances are
known and permitted by God.
He is using them as tools to build
our relationships with Him. He
turns all of them for our good
when we allow Him to work in our
lives—when we love, obey,
and trust Him.

DR. CHARLES F. STANLEY

 Let us draw near with confidence to the
throne of grace, so that we may receive mercy
and find grace to help in time of need.

—HEBREWS 4:16

You may not be able to
understand all that God does in
your life. But when you can focus
on the truth that He is sovereign,
you will find some blessing
and value in everything
you go through.

DR. CHARLES F. STANLEY

We do not lose heart, but though our outer man is decaying, yet our inner
man is being renewed day by day. For momentary, light affliction is producing
for us an eternal weight of glory far beyond all comparison, while we look not at
the things which are seen, but at the things which are not seen; for the things
which are seen are temporal, but the things which are not seen are eternal.

—2 CORINTHIANS 4:16-18

It doesn't make any difference how many broken pieces your life is in. In His sovereignty and wisdom, Jesus knows exactly how to put them together. Christ your Savior makes your life worthwhile now and for all eternity.

DR. CHARLES F. STANLEY

Now to Him who is able to keep you from stumbling, and to make you stand in the presence of His glory blameless with great joy, to the only God our Savior, through Jesus Christ our Lord, be glory, majesty, dominion and authority, before all time and now and forever. Amen.

—JUDE v. 24-25

Anything you hold too tightly, you will lose.

*"Beware, and be on your guard against every
form of greed; for not even when one has an
abundance does his life consist of his possessions."*

—LUKE 12:15

Many people are wrapped up
in themselves and their own
interests. All they talk about is
what they're going to do and what
they're going to accumulate and
possess. But God says if that's the
way you're living, you're a fool.
You're going to lose.

DR. CHARLES F. STANLEY

Do nothing from selfishness or empty conceit, but with
humility of mind regard one another as more important
than yourselves; do not merely look out for your own
personal interests, but also for the interests of others.

—PHILIPPIANS 2:3-4

Whenever we leave God out of the issues of our lives, it's going to cost us. We make wrong decisions because of human nature, our erroneous ideas, and our faulty perceptions of our circumstances. We take roads that are not the Father's will for us, and the next thing we know we've created more problems and made our situations a great deal worse.

DR. CHARLES F. STANLEY

There is a way which seems right to a man, but its end is the way of death.

—PROVERBS 16:25

Some people demand their rights.
But where in the Bible does it say
we have rights? God is sovereign—
He even decides when we live
and when we die. We don't have
any rights other than what
He gives to us.

DR. CHARLES F. STANLEY

 "Woe to the one who quarrels with his Maker—
an earthenware vessel among the vessels of earth!
Will the clay say to the potter, 'What are you doing?'"

—ISAIAH 45:9

Our source of freedom is not
found in a government.
The true source of our liberty
is through a relationship with
Jesus Christ.

DR. CHARLES F. STANLEY

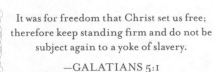

It was for freedom that Christ set us free;
therefore keep standing firm and do not be
subject again to a yoke of slavery.

—GALATIANS 5:1

People think that money is what really matters. But only God matters. Wealth comes and goes— Jesus will never leave you. Once you receive Him as your Savior, you have all the security you need in the world.

DR. CHARLES F. STANLEY

 The world is passing away, and also its lusts; but the one who does the will of God lives forever.

—1 JOHN 2:17

Whatever comes between you and God is an idol—and He will target it because He sees it as competition. It is a barrier to His will being done in your life.

DR. CHARLES F. STANLEY

"Watch yourselves, that you do not forget the covenant of the LORD your God which He made with you, and make for yourselves a graven image in the form of anything against which the LORD your God has commanded you. For the LORD your God is a consuming fire, a jealous God."

—DEUTERONOMY 4:23-24

Disappointments are inevitable, and discouragement is a choice.

My tears have been my food day and night, while they say to me all day long, "Where is your God?" These things I remember and I pour out my soul within me . . . . Why are you in despair, O my soul? And why have you become disturbed within me? Hope in God, for I shall again praise Him for the help of His presence.

—PSALM 42:3–5

If you want to overcome your discouragement, you need to realize it doesn't help to rehash its start or what caused it. You must change your viewpoint. Look to God. Think about what He's done for you—the countless ways He's proven Himself faithful through the years. Consider what He is doing in your life right now—how He is providing for you and revealing Himself to you. Then look ahead. Claim His promises for the future.

DR. CHARLES F. STANLEY

Remember my affliction and my wandering, the wormwood and bitterness. Surely my soul remembers and is bowed down within me. This I recall to my mind, therefore I have hope. The LORD's lovingkindnesses indeed never cease, for His compassions never fail. They are new every morning; great is Your faithfulness.

—LAMENTATIONS 3:19-23

God doesn't change. He's rescued
me in the past, so He can deliver me
from any difficulty I am presently
facing. And He can take me
where He wants me to go.

DR. CHARLES F. STANLEY

Be gracious to me, O God, be gracious to me, for my soul takes refuge
in You; and in the shadow of Your wings I will take refuge until destruction
passes by. I will cry to God Most High, to God who accomplishes all things
for me. He will send from heaven and save me; He reproaches him who
tramples upon me. God will send forth His lovingkindness and His truth.

—PSALM 57:1-3

Remember the acrostic H.A.L.T. It means you should avoid becoming too hungry, angry, lonely, or tired. Why? Simply because that is when you will get discouraged and are in danger of making some very costly decisions.

DR. CHARLES F. STANLEY

"Come to Me, all who are weary and heavy-laden, and I will give you rest. Take My yoke upon you and learn from Me, for I am gentle and humble in heart, and you will find rest for your souls. For My yoke is easy and My burden is light."

—MATTHEW 11:28-30

When you choose to remain discouraged, you will begin to question the Lord. You will think, *God isn't answering my prayers. He isn't doing anything to help me. He must not care for me.* Little by little, Satan interjects doubt until you drift in your relationship with the Father. Meanwhile, the Holy Spirit remains within you—faithfully giving you direction, strength, encouragement, and whatever else is needed for you to become the person He wants you to be. However, you must choose to heed His promptings.

DR. CHARLES F. STANLEY

 "The LORD is the one who goes ahead of you; He will be with you. He will not fail you or forsake you. Do not fear or be dismayed."

—DEUTERONOMY 31:8

When you get so prideful that you will not do the dirty, lowly jobs, then you're in a mess. God may be trying to teach you something. Your greatest impact may very well be through humble service.

DR. CHARLES F. STANLEY

 A man's pride will bring him low, but a humble spirit will obtain honor.

—PROVERBS 29:23

No matter what has caused your discouragement, God—with all of His power, goodness, wisdom, and love—is going to direct you to victory if you will listen to Him. He will turn this time of discouragement into something very beneficial in your life.

DR. CHARLES F. STANLEY

Thanks be to God, who gives us the victory through our Lord Jesus Christ. Therefore, my beloved brethren, be steadfast, immovable, always abounding in the work of the Lord, knowing that your toil is not in vain in the Lord.

—1 CORINTHIANS 15:57-58

Obedience always brings blessing.

Who may ascend into the hill of the LORD? And who may stand in His holy place? He who has clean hands and a pure heart, who has not lifted up his soul to falsehood and has not sworn deceitfully. He shall receive a blessing from the LORD and righteousness from the God of his salvation.

—PSALM 24:3-5

A blessing is anything that
can be categorized as an
expression of God's goodness
and love toward us.

DR. CHARLES F. STANLEY

Blessed be the God and Father of our Lord Jesus
Christ, who has blessed us with every spiritual
blessing in the heavenly places in Christ.

— EPHESIANS 1:3

You may be thinking, *I've been obedient, and I've been praying, but I don't feel blessed.* It may very well be that you've overlooked something important. The blessings God sends don't always take the form you expect. It depends on your situation. At times, the Holy Spirit will give you an awesome sense of peace. It may be that He gives you an overwhelming joy or an incredible feeling of contentment. Many people never think about peace, joy, and contentment as blessings, but they are.

DR. CHARLES F. STANLEY

 The LORD bless you, and keep you; the LORD make His face shine on you, and be gracious to you; the LORD lift up His countenance on you, and give you peace.

— NUMBERS 6:24-26

An intimate relationship with God is the most valuable thing you and I will ever possess. Out of this intimate relationship flows everything in your life—how you think, what you have, what you receive, how you walk, and how you live your life. Your relationship with God is that important.

DR. CHARLES F. STANLEY

"This is eternal life, that they may know You, the only true God, and Jesus Christ whom You have sent."

—JOHN 17:3

Do you believe God is omniscient—all-knowing? Do you trust He loves you unconditionally? Do you have faith that He knows what is best for you? If that is the case, shouldn't you accept that what He is doing in your life—regardless of how it appears right now—will most likely lead to an awesome blessing for you? Sometimes we don't see it that way, but it is the truth.

DR. CHARLES F. STANLEY

"Blessed are you who hunger now, for you shall be satisfied. Blessed are you who weep now, for you shall laugh. Blessed are you when men hate you, and ostracize you, and insult you, and scorn your name as evil, for the sake of the Son of Man. Be glad in that day and leap for joy, for behold, your reward is great in heaven."

—LUKE 6:21-23

One of God's goals is to bring us to the end of ourselves. You and I are most useful when we are absolutely, totally dependent upon the Father.

DR. CHARLES F. STANLEY

"Do not fear! Stand by and see the salvation of the LORD which He will accomplish for you today . . . . The LORD will fight for you while you keep silent."

— EXODUS 14:13-14

God has a plan for you. It's your personal pathway of faith. No one else can walk it but you because it has your name on it. You were created to travel it; and if you will walk down the center of that road in obedience to Him, you will most certainly be blessed.

DR. CHARLES F. STANLEY

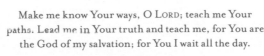

Make me know Your ways, O LORD; teach me Your paths. Lead me in Your truth and teach me, for You are the God of my salvation; for You I wait all the day.

—PSALM 25:4-5

To walk in the Spirit is to obey the initial promptings of the Spirit.

Walk by the Spirit, and you will not carry out the desire of the flesh. . . . If we live by the Spirit, let us also walk by the Spirit.

—GALATIANS 5:16, 25

You cannot interpret the Word
of God properly, you cannot
live a godly life, and you cannot
serve the Lord adequately apart
from the power of the Holy Spirit
working in you.

DR. CHARLES F. STANLEY

"You will receive power when the Holy Spirit has
come upon you; and you shall be My witnesses
both in Jerusalem, and in all Judea and Samaria,
and even to the remotest part of the earth."

—ACTS 1:8

There are three persons of the Trinity. God the Father, Son, and Holy Spirit are intimately and actively involved with all creation. The Father does His work. The Son does His work. The Spirit does His work. Each has a vital role in every believer's life.

DR. CHARLES F. STANLEY

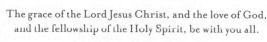

The grace of the Lord Jesus Christ, and the love of God, and the fellowship of the Holy Spirit, be with you all.

—2 CORINTHIANS 13:14

The Holy Spirit is not a force. He is as much a Person as Jesus is. He is the One who walks beside us, our Helper and Comforter. He is the One who gives us assurance of our relationships to the Father. He testifies to each believer, "You are one of God's children. You have been adopted into the kingdom forever."

DR. CHARLES F. STANLEY

All who are being led by the Spirit of God, these are sons of God. For you have not received a spirit of slavery leading to fear again, but you have received a spirit of adoption as sons by which we cry out, "Abba! Father!" The Spirit Himself testifies with our spirit that we are children of God.

—ROMANS 8:14-16

It is the authority, power,
and unction of the Holy Spirit
that teaches through a Sunday
school teacher, pastor, musician,
or evangelist. God intends for
all of us to do our work in His
wisdom, energy, and strength and
by His authority.

DR. CHARLES F. STANLEY

"When the Helper comes, whom I will send to you
from the Father, that is the Spirit of truth who proceeds
from the Father, He will testify about Me, and you will
testify also, because you have been with Me
from the beginning."

—JOHN 15:26–27

Every morning, you wake up to three enemies—the world, the flesh, and the devil. How do you handle these enemies? You must be filled with the Holy Spirit— listening to and walking with Him moment by moment.

DR. CHARLES F. STANLEY

Our struggle is not against flesh and blood, but against the rulers, against the powers, against the world forces of this darkness, against the spiritual forces of wickedness in the heavenly places. Therefore, take up the full armor of God, so that you will be able to resist in the evil day, and having done everything, to stand firm.

—EPHESIANS 6:12-13

Every one of us has two battles to fight when tempted. First, there is the struggle in our minds. Second, there is the conflict with our behaviors. If we don't win the battle for our minds, we will not be godly in our behaviors because our minds govern everything we do. Therefore, we must train our minds to yield to the initial promptings of the Spirit.

DR. CHARLES F. STANLEY

Those who are according to the flesh set their minds on the things of the flesh, but those who are according to the Spirit, the things of the Spirit. For the mind set on the flesh is death, but the mind set on the Spirit is life and peace.

—ROMANS 8:5-6

You can never outgive God.

"Give, and it will be given to you. They will pour into your lap a good measure—pressed down, shaken together, and running over. For by your standard of measure it will be measured to you in return."

—LUKE 6:38

Ideas can change, but biblical principles do not—they stay the same. They are steady and reliable because God does not change.

DR. CHARLES F. STANLEY

Jesus Christ is the same yesterday and today and forever.

—HEBREWS 13:8

Everything you and I have comes from God's hand. Every copper penny in our pockets, our abilities, skills, talents, gifts—everything originates with Him. And we are called to be managers, stewards, and caretakers of the things He has provided for us.

DR. CHARLES F. STANLEY

 Every good thing given and every perfect gift is
from above, coming down from the Father of lights,
with whom there is no variation or shifting shadow.

—JAMES 1:17

When people leave God out
of their finances, they're going to
have problems. Where does God
fit into our finances? Where He
should be in every aspect of our
lives—at the very center.

DR. CHARLES F. STANLEY

"Remember the LORD your God,
for it is He who is giving you power
to make wealth."

—DEUTERONOMY 8:18

God created the galaxies. He can write anything He wishes in the heavens. So why did He decide not to do so, choosing instead to spread His message of salvation through people? Simply because He loves us so much He wanted to give us the privilege, honor, and joy of sharing the truth of the gospel with those around us.

DR. CHARLES F. STANLEY

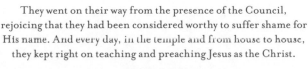

They went on their way from the presence of the Council, rejoicing that they had been considered worthy to suffer shame for His name. And every day, in the temple and from house to house, they kept right on teaching and preaching Jesus as the Christ.

—ACTS 5:41-42

If you're willing to trust the Savior with your eternity, surely you can trust Him with one penny out of every dime.

DR. CHARLES F. STANLEY

 "Bring the whole tithe into the storehouse, so that there may be food in My house, and test Me now in this," says the LORD of hosts, "if I will not open for you the windows of heaven and pour out for you a blessing until it overflows." —MALACHI 3:10

In more than fifty years as a pastor, no one has ever come to me and said, "I started tithing and I went broke." Or, "I began tithing and I have less now than I've ever had before." Not one person. This is because by His very nature, God cannot do otherwise than bless you when you obey Him— whether it is your finances or any other area of your life. Take Him at His Word, and watch Him work.

DR. CHARLES F. STANLEY

"Behold, we have left our own homes and followed You."
And He said to them, "Truly I say to you, there is no one who has left house or wife or brothers or parents or children, for the sake of the kingdom of God, who will not receive many times as much at this time and in the age to come, eternal life."
—LUKE 18:28-30

To live the Christian life is to allow Jesus to live His life in and through us.

The mystery which has been hidden from the past ages and generations, but has now been manifested to His saints . . . which is Christ in you, the hope of glory. We proclaim Him, admonishing every man and teaching every man with all wisdom, so that we may present every man complete in Christ.

—COLOSSIANS 1:26-28

Would it shock you if I said I couldn't live this Christian life? It is the truth. One of the happiest days of my life was when I discovered I couldn't live this life on my own. God knew I couldn't and showed me it was okay.

DR. CHARLES F. STANLEY

 "Abide in Me, and I in you. As the branch cannot bear fruit of itself unless it abides in the vine, so neither can you unless you abide in Me."

—JOHN 15:4

Baptism symbolizes dying to our
old ways of life and rising to walk
in the newness of life in Christ.
Gone are our dead spirits.
Now we have the living Spirit
of Jesus dwelling within us.

DR. CHARLES F. STANLEY

Do you not know that all of us who have been baptized into
Christ Jesus have been baptized into His death? Therefore
we have been buried with Him through baptism into death,
so that as Christ was raised from the dead through the glory
of the Father, so we too might walk in newness of life.

—ROMANS 6:3-4

What is sanctification? God
sets you apart to live for Him all
the days of your life, to be fruitful
and become more like Him.
However, it is a process that is
not complete until we are with
Him in heaven.

DR. CHARLES F. STANLEY

Now we see in a mirror dimly, but then face to
face; now I know in part, but then I will know
fully just as I also have been fully known.

—1 CORINTHIANS 13:12

The Christian life is not about what we have to do—what God requires us to achieve. The Christian life is about what Jesus is doing in us. He knew we couldn't accomplish His goals for us on our own—and we shouldn't. That would only draw attention to ourselves. But when He works in us in a supernatural way, He alone is glorified.

DR. CHARLES F. STANLEY

"I have been crucified with Christ; and it is no longer I who live, but Christ lives in me; and the life which I now live in the flesh I live by faith in the Son of God, who loved me and gave Himself up for me."

—GALATIANS 2:20

Jesus is never going to leave you. He set up housekeeping in your life the moment you trusted Him as Savior, so He is there to stay forever. This is why you cannot return to being lost once He has saved you. If the living God is dwelling within you, who or what could possibly remove Him?

DR. CHARLES F. STANLEY

It is a trustworthy statement: For if we died with Him, we will also live with Him; if we endure, we will also reign with Him; if we deny Him, He also will deny us; if we are faithless, He remains faithful, for He cannot deny Himself.

—2 TIMOTHY 2:11-13

What is a saint? A saint is a
person who has been redeemed
by the blood of Jesus Christ and
in whom and through whom He
dwells. This is what makes the
difference between the rest of the
world and us. God in the person
of the Holy Spirit is living His
life in us. That's what makes us
unique—what makes us saints.

DR. CHARLES F. STANLEY

Through Him we both have our access in one Spirit to the Father. So then
you are no longer strangers and aliens, but you are fellow citizens with the
saints, and are of God's household, having been built on the foundation of
the apostles and prophets, Christ Jesus Himself being the corner stone.

—EPHESIANS 2:18-20

God blesses us so that we might bless others.

Instruct those who are rich in this present world not to be conceited or to fix their hope on the uncertainty of riches, but on God, who richly supplies us with all things to enjoy. Instruct them to do good, to be rich in good works, to be generous and ready to share.

—1 TIMOTHY 6:17-18

What does it mean for God
to bless others through us?
It means He intervenes in other
people's lives through our
willingness to help them and to
meet their emotional, material,
or spiritual needs as He directs.

DR. CHARLES F. STANLEY

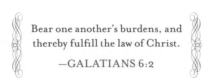

Bear one another's burdens, and
thereby fulfill the law of Christ.

—GALATIANS 6:2

We are the body of Christ.
We are to be the hands, feet,
eyes, and ears of our Lord Jesus
Christ who is seated at the
Father's right hand.

DR. CHARLES F. STANLEY

He gave some as apostles, and some as prophets, and
some as evangelists, and some as pastors and teachers,
for the equipping of the saints for the work of service,
to the building up of the body of Christ.

—EPHESIANS 4:11-12

The Father saves us and indwells us by His Spirit to conform us to the likeness of Christ so that each of us will be a walking, living example of Jesus Christ. We are expressions of His goodness, love, and mercy.

DR. CHARLES F. STANLEY

Those whom He foreknew, He also predestined to become conformed to the image of His Son, so that He would be the firstborn among many brethren.

—ROMANS 8:29

The happiest people I know are
those who are generous and give
of themselves, who have a servant
spirit. When you get right with
God, you naturally want to give.

DR. CHARLES F. STANLEY

"Help the weak and remember the words
of the Lord Jesus, that He Himself said,
'It is more blessed to give than to receive.'"

—ACTS 20:35

Fervent love expresses itself both in words and deeds. Therefore, genuinely love other people. Give yourself away to them in such a manner they will truly experience the unconditional love of God.

DR. CHARLES F. STANLEY

"By this all men will know that you are My disciples, if you have love for one another."

—JOHN 13:35

When you arrive in heaven
and stand before the Lord, you
will not be rewarded for what
you've received. You will only be
rewarded for what you've given.

DR. CHARLES F. STANLEY

"Come, you who are blessed of My Father, inherit the kingdom prepared
for you from the foundation of the world. For I was hungry, and you gave
Me something to eat; I was thirsty, and you gave Me something to drink;
I was a stranger, and you invited Me in; naked, and you clothed Me; I was
sick, and you visited Me; I was in prison, and you came to Me."
—MATTHEW 25:34-36

Adversity is a bridge to a deeper relationship with God.

I count all things to be loss in view of the surpassing value of knowing Christ Jesus my Lord, for whom I have suffered the loss of all things, and count them but rubbish so that I may gain Christ, and may be found in Him, not having a righteousness of my own derived from the Law, but that which is through faith in Christ, the righteousness which comes from God on the basis of faith, that I may know Him and the power of His resurrection and the fellowship of His sufferings, being conformed to His death; in order that I may attain to the resurrection from the dead.

—PHILIPPIANS 3:8-10

What makes the difference in everything you face is your attitude. Adversity can be a heavy, overwhelming burden that makes you weary, restless, and desperate. Or you can see it as an opportunity, a bridge over which you can travel above your circumstances and into a deeper relationship with Jesus Christ.

DR. CHARLES F. STANLEY

In this you greatly rejoice, even though now for a little while, if necessary, you have been distressed by various trials, so that the proof of your faith, being more precious than gold which is perishable, even though tested by fire, may be found to result in praise and glory and honor at the revelation of Jesus Christ.

—1 PETER 1:6–7

When I am at my weakest moments, when I think I just can't keep going, I get the greatest surge of supernatural energy and power in my life by spending time in God's presence. I can keep going because my relationship with Him gives me a sense of sufficiency and hope. I know He's promised to guide me, keep me, and supply my needs—whatever they may be.

DR. CHARLES F. STANLEY

The righteous cry, and the LORD hears and delivers them out of all their troubles. The LORD is near to the brokenhearted and saves those who are crushed in spirit. Many are the afflictions of the righteous, but the LORD delivers him out of them all.

—PSALM 34:17-19

Adversity can be a gift. It can be a blessing from Almighty God to prepare us for what He is calling us to do. We're so valuable to Him that He does whatever it takes to equip us to become who He created us to be—powerful servants of the living God.

DR. CHARLES F. STANLEY

"I will bring the third part through the fire, refine them as silver is refined, and test them as gold is tested. They will call on My name, and I will answer them; I will say, 'They are My people,' and they will say, 'The LORD is my God.'"

—ZECHARIAH 13:9

Difficulty, hardship, and pain strengthen your faith and deepen your message. You understand more and you're more effective in what you have to say to others because of how God has worked in your life. He equips you to comfort others.

DR. CHARLES F. STANLEY

Blessed be the God and Father of our Lord Jesus Christ, the Father of mercies and God of all comfort, who comforts us in all our affliction so that we will be able to comfort those who are in any affliction with the comfort with which we ourselves are comforted by God. For just as the sufferings of Christ are ours in abundance, so also our comfort is abundant through Christ. But if we are afflicted, it is for your comfort and salvation; or if we are comforted, it is for your comfort.

—2 CORINTHIANS 1:3-6

Learn to see everything as coming from God. This is a basic principle that will prevent you from becoming bitter, resentful, and hostile.

DR. CHARLES F. STANLEY

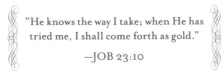

"He knows the way I take; when He has tried me, I shall come forth as gold."

—JOB 23:10

There are two big rails on the bridge of adversity. The first is that God is in control of everything. The second is that He is going to turn every circumstance for your good. Hold on tight to these two truths, and you can overcome any challenge or problem—no matter what it is.

DR. CHARLES F. STANLEY

Thanks be to God, who always leads us in triumph in Christ, and manifests through us the sweet aroma of the knowledge of Him in every place.

—2 CORINTHIANS 2:14

Prayer is life's greatest time saver.

Be careful how you walk, not as unwise men but as wise,
making the most of your time, because the days are evil.

—EPHESIANS 5:15-16

Time is precious. It is the substance that makes up your life, and God has only given you a specific amount. You don't know how long it's going to last, so you need to make the most of it.

DR. CHARLES F. STANLEY

Teach us to number our days, that we may present to You a heart of wisdom.

—PSALM 90:12

What you and I do with our lives is very important. We either invest them wisely or we waste them. The truth is, to squander time—to misspend our lives—is a sin against God.

DR. CHARLES F. STANLEY

Who is the man who desires life and loves length of days that he may see good? Keep your tongue from evil and your lips from speaking deceit. Depart from evil and do good; seek peace and pursue it. The eyes of the LORD are toward the righteous and His ears are open to their cry.

—PSALM 34:12-15

If out of seven days a week,
twenty-four hours a day, a person
cannot give at least an hour
and a half of his time to focus
on and worship God, that
person is distorted in his
thinking and lacking in real,
genuine spirituality.

DR. CHARLES F. STANLEY

 Ascribe to the LORD the glory due His name; bring
an offering, and come before Him; worship the LORD
in holy array. Tremble before Him, all the earth.

—1 CHRONICLES 16:29-30

God has given every one of us enough time to seek Him and do His will each day. You have enough time to pray, read His Word, worship Him, and serve Him. Because He is wise and omniscient, He knows exactly what you and I need. Therefore, He would never require you to do anything He didn't give you enough time to do.

DR. CHARLES F. STANLEY

He has made everything appropriate in its time. He has also set eternity in their heart, yet so that man will not find out the work which God has done from the beginning even to the end. . . . I know that everything God does will remain forever; there is nothing to add to it and there is nothing to take from it, for God has so worked that men should fear Him.

—ECCLESIASTES 3:11, 14

The best way to make your life the most productive it can be is by starting your day being quiet, listening to God, and reading His Word. He knows how to direct you, ready you for emergencies, and keep you from wrong decisions that will result in costly delays and long-range repercussions. Give Him time to change your plans.

DR. CHARLES F. STANLEY

To You, O LORD, I lift up my soul. O my God, in You I trust, do not let me be ashamed; do not let my enemies exult over me. Indeed, none of those who wait for You will be ashamed.

—PSALM 25:1-3

Because you're a believer, the Spirit of God communicates to your subconscious mind. At night you may pray, "Lord, show me what to do. I want You to confirm I'm heading in the right direction. If I ever stray from Your will, please stop me." He wants to show you the right thing to do, so even as you sleep, the Holy Spirit is working things out within you, giving you His viewpoint on your circumstances.

DR. CHARLES F. STANLEY

Be anxious for nothing, but in everything by prayer and supplication with thanksgiving let your requests be made known to God. And the peace of God, which surpasses all comprehension, will guard your hearts and your minds in Christ Jesus.

—PHILIPPIANS 4:6-7

No Christian has ever been called to "go it alone" in his or her walk of faith.

Let us consider how to stimulate one another to love and good deeds, not forsaking our own assembling together, as is the habit of some, but encouraging one another; and all the more as you see the day drawing near.

—HEBREWS 10:24-25

Throughout history, all kinds of "isms" have come and gone. But the church is still here, growing by leaps and bounds around the world. Why? Simply because it is His church—His body through which He works.

DR. CHARLES F. STANLEY

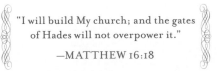

"I will build My church; and the gates of Hades will not overpower it."

—MATTHEW 16:18

Why did Christ establish the
church? To give us guidance and
direction for our lives; to provide
strength, protection, and help
in times of difficulty, hardship,
suffering, and sorrow; and to be
His representative to a lost
and dying world.

DR. CHARLES F. STANLEY

God was in Christ reconciling the world to Himself, not counting
their trespasses against them, and He has committed to us the
word of reconciliation. Therefore, we are ambassadors for Christ,
as though God were making an appeal through us; we beg you on
behalf of Christ, be reconciled to God.

—2 CORINTHIANS 5:19-20

What is worship? It is honoring God for who He is. We sing, praise the Lord, recall His blessings, and give Him thanks for the good things He's done for us. We pray, read His Word, give our offerings in obedience to Him. And we fellowship with each other—grateful for how He is working in each of our lives.

DR. CHARLES F. STANLEY

 Come, let us worship and bow down, let us kneel before the LORD our Maker. For He is our God, and we are the people of His pasture.

—PSALM 95:6-7

One of the wonderful things about Scripture is that you'll never exhaust it. You can study it for a thousand years, and God will still speak through it.

DR. CHARLES F. STANLEY

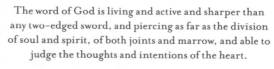

The word of God is living and active and sharper than any two-edged sword, and piercing as far as the division of soul and spirit, of both joints and marrow, and able to judge the thoughts and intentions of the heart.

—HEBREWS 4:12

What is it that keeps us straight,
heading in the right direction?
What keeps our hearts pure and
protects us from the world's ideas?
It's the people of God.
We are accountable to each other
and responsible for protecting
each other with the Word of God.

DR. CHARLES F. STANLEY

Preach the word; be ready in season and out of season;
reprove, rebuke, exhort, with great patience and instruction. . . .
Be sober in all things, endure hardship, do the work
of an evangelist, fulfill your ministry.

—2 TIMOTHY 4:2, 5

God has given every one of
His children a spiritual gift that
is to be exercised for the benefit
of the Body of Christ. He's gifted
you—not for yourself, but to
bless others.

DR. CHARLES F. STANLEY

There are varieties of gifts, but the same Spirit. And there are varieties
of ministries, and the same Lord. There are varieties of effects, but
the same God who works all things in all persons. But to each one is
given the manifestation of the Spirit for the common good.

—I CORINTHIANS 12:4-7

We learn more in our valley experiences than on our mountaintops.

Even though I walk through the valley of the shadow of death, I fear no evil, for You are with me; Your rod and Your staff, they comfort me. . . . Surely goodness and lovingkindness will follow me all the days of my life, and I will dwell in the house of the LORD forever.

—PSALM 23:4, 6

There's no such thing as living continually on the mountaintop, where there's uninterrupted success, happiness, joy, and prosperity. All of us will experience times when we find ourselves in the valley, when our paths are lined with difficulty and hardship. But remember, because of God, there is always hope in the valley.

DR. CHARLES F. STANLEY

Beloved, do not be surprised at the fiery ordeal among you, which comes upon you for your testing, as though some strange thing were happening to you; but to the degree that you share the sufferings of Christ, keep on rejoicing, so that also at the revelation of His glory you may rejoice with exultation.

—1 PETER 4:12-13

Jesus told us He is our Good Shepherd—and sometimes the Good Shepherd will lead us into valley experiences where we hurt, where there's pain and suffering. But He takes us there to get us ready for the next mountain peak—for even greater blessings and higher levels of intimacy and service.

DR. CHARLES F. STANLEY

 He shepherded them according to the integrity of his heart, and guided them with his skillful hands.

—PSALM 78:72

God always has a higher purpose in mind than just keeping us happy.

DR. CHARLES F. STANLEY

The kingdom of God is not eating and drinking, but righteousness and peace and joy in the Holy Spirit. For he who in this way serves Christ is acceptable to God and approved by men. So then we pursue the things which make for peace and the building up of one another.

—ROMANS 14:17-19

The Father has the very best plans for us. Although He allows every one of us to go through valleys, He never intends to leave us there. Valley living is not the plan of God for His children. It is a passageway, not a destination.

DR. CHARLES F. STANLEY

How blessed is the man whose strength is in You, in whose heart are the highways to Zion! Passing through the valley of Baca they make it a spring; the early rain also covers it with blessings. They go from strength to strength, every one of them appears before God in Zion.

—PSALM 84:5-7

Do you sense God's presence with you? Or do you think He is out yonder somewhere? If you feel He's distant, then you don't truly understand who He is in your life. He is the Good Shepherd, the One who is always there for you.

DR. CHARLES F. STANLEY

Like a shepherd He will tend His flock, in His arm He will gather the lambs and carry them in His bosom; He will gently lead the nursing ewes.

—ISAIAH 40:11

The trials we endure can be excruciating, beyond what we think we can endure. But there is a purifying work that only pain can do in our lives—refining us, showing us what is really important, helping us rely solely on God. We realize the only thing that really matters is that He has His way in our lives.

DR. CHARLES F. STANLEY

I pray that the eyes of your heart may be enlightened, so that you will know what is the hope of His calling, what are the riches of the glory of His inheritance in the saints, and what is the surpassing greatness of His power toward us who believe. These are in accordance with the working of the strength of His might which He brought about in Christ, when He raised Him from the dead.

—EPHESIANS 1:18-20

An eager anticipation of the Lord's return keeps us living productively.

We are children of God, and it has not appeared as yet what we will be. We know that when He appears, we will be like Him, because we will see Him just as He is. And everyone who has this hope fixed on Him purifies himself, just as He is pure.

—1 JOHN 3:2-3

The next event on God's calendar
is that He will return for His
church. What has to take place
before Jesus comes again?
The answer is nothing. His
return is imminent.

DR. CHARLES F. STANLEY

The Lord Himself will descend from heaven with a shout, with
the voice of the archangel and with the trumpet of God, and the
dead in Christ will rise first. Then we who are alive and remain
will be caught up together with them in the clouds to meet the
Lord in the air, and so we shall always be with the Lord.

—I THESSALONIANS 4:16-17

If you knew Jesus would come
back tomorrow, would you want
to change anything about your
life? Is there anyone you need to
forgive or lead to salvation?
If you are truly persuaded He
could return at any moment, then
you should be motivated to make
those changes right now. Live
every day of your life conscious
that you could meet the Lord.

DR. CHARLES F. STANLEY

"Be on the alert, for you do not know which day your Lord is coming. But be
sure of this, that if the head of the house had known at what time of the night
the thief was coming, he would have been on the alert and would not have
allowed his house to be broken into. For this reason you also must be ready; for
the Son of Man is coming at an hour when you do not think He will."

—MATTHEW 24:42-44

Prophesies in Scripture are like mountain ranges. You can see them lined up one after another like a series—and you know there's distance between them because of the mist, but you cannot tell exactly how far it is.

DR. CHARLES F. STANLEY

"Heaven and earth will pass away, but My words will not pass away. But of that day or hour no one knows, not even the angels in heaven, nor the Son, but the Father alone. Take heed, keep on the alert; for you do not know when the appointed time will come."

—MARK 13:31-33

As the children of God,
we should be faithfully watching
for Christ's return. We should also
be telling others the truth of the
gospel so people worldwide
can be saved.

DR. CHARLES F. STANLEY

 "This gospel of the kingdom shall be preached
in the whole world as a testimony to all the
nations, and then the end will come."

—MATTHEW 24:14

The more truth you and I understand, the more we're able to stand strong before people who mock and criticize us. So many people use the most precious name in all of eternity—the name of our Lord Jesus—as slang or profanity. But as believers, we are to stand fast, knowing His name is above every other.

DR. CHARLES F. STANLEY

 "Great and marvelous are Your works, O Lord God, the Almighty; righteous and true are Your ways, King of the nations! Who will not fear, O Lord, and glorify Your name? For You alone are holy; FOR ALL THE NATIONS WILL COME AND WORSHIP BEFORE YOU, FOR YOUR RIGHTEOUS ACTS HAVE BEEN REVEALED."

—REVELATION 15:3-4

You don't have to preach, sing,
or go to the mission field to serve
God. But you are responsible
to obey Him out of love and
devotion—to live a godly life and
serve Him until the day you take
your last breath or He returns.
Make every moment count until
you see Him face to face. That,
my friend, is life at its best.

DR. CHARLES F. STANLEY

The Spirit and the bride say, "Come." And let the one who hears
say, "Come." And let the one who is thirsty come; let the one who
wishes take the water of life without cost. . . . He who testifies to
these things says, "Yes, I am coming quickly." Amen. Come, Lord
Jesus. The grace of the Lord Jesus be with all. Amen.

—REVELATION 22:17, 20-21